Learning Short-take®

PERSUASIVE
PRESENTATION
SKILLS

Create, prepare and design with confidence

CATHERINE MATTISKE

TPC - The Performance Company Pty Ltd
Level 20, Darling Park
Tower 2, 201 Sussex Street,
Sydney NSW 2000
Australia

ACN 077 455 273
email: tpc@tpc.net.au
Website: www.catherinemattiske.com

© TPC – The Performance Company Pty Limited
First edition published in 2006
Second edition published in 2011
Third edition published in 2022

All rights reserved. Apart from any fair dealing for the purposes of study, research or review, as permitted under Australian copyright law, no part of this publication may be reproduced by any means without the written permission of the copyright owner. Every effort has been made to obtain permission relating to information reproduced in this publication.

The information in this publication is based on the current state of commercial and industry practice, applicable legislation, general law and the general circumstances as at the date of publication. No person shall rely on any of the contents of this publication and the publisher and the author expressly exclude all liability for direct and indirect loss suffered by any person resulting in any way from the use of or reliance on this publication or any part of it. Any options and advice are offered solely in pursuance of the author's and the publisher's intention to provide information, and have not been specifically sought.

For eBook version: By payment of the required fees, you have been granted the non-exclusive, non-transferable right to access and read the text of this e-book on screen. No part of this text may be reproduced, transmitted, downloaded, decompiled, reverse engineered, or stored in or introduced into any information storage retrieval system, in any form or by any means, whether the electronic or mechanical, now known or hereinafter invented, without the express permission of the author.

A catalogue record for this book is available from the National Library of Australia

National Library of Australia
Cataloguing-in-Publication data

Mattiske, Catherine
Persuasive Presentation Skills: Create, Prepare and Design with Confidence

ISBN 978-1-921547-04-1

1. Occupational training 2. Learning I. Title

370.113

Distributed by TPC - The Performance Company - www.catherinemattiske.com
For further information contact TPC - The Performance Company, Sydney Australia on +61 (02) 9555 1953.

HELLO.

Welcome to the Learning Short-take® process!

This Learning Short-take® is a bite sized learning package that aims to improve your skills and provide you with an opportunity for personal and professional development to achieve success in your role.

This Learning Short-take® combines self study with workplace activities in a unique learning system to keep you motivated and energized.
So let's get started!

Step 1:
What's inside?

- Learning Short-take®. This section contains all of the learning content and will guide you through the learning process.
- Learning Activities. You will be prompted to complete these as you read through.
- Learning Journal. This is a summary of your key learnings. Update it when prompted.
- Skill Development Action Plan. Learning is about taking action. This is your action plan where you'll plan how you will implement your learning.

Step 2:
Complete the Learning Short-take®

- Learning Short-takes® are best completed in a quiet environment that is free of distractions.
- Schedule time in your calendar to complete the Learning Short-take® and prioritize this time as an investment in your own professional development.
- Depending on the title, most participants complete the Learning Short-take® from 90 minutes to 2.5 hours.

Step 3:
Meet with your Manager/Coach

- Schedule a 30 minute meeting with your Manager or Coach.
- At this meeting share your completed Activities, Learning Journal and Skill Development Action Plan.
- Most importantly, discuss and agree on how you will implement your learning in your role.

GET VIP ACCESS
TO YOUR MATERIALS

This Learning Short-take® includes an interactive activity book, associated tools and job aids, plus a bonus eBook.

1 Visit
https://www.catherinemattiske.com/books

2 Select your book

3 Click: **VIP ACCESS**

4 Enter the code: PPS2022319

WELCOME

Persuasive Presentation Skills
Create, Prepare and Design with Confidence

Persuasive Presentation Skills combines self-study with realistic workplace activities to provide presenters with the key skills and techniques to prepare and deliver dynamic presentations. After assessing your current approach to preparing and delivering presentations, **Persuasive Presentation Skills** will help you develop unique and innovative strategies to improve your presentation success from small meetings to large audiences. You will learn to effectively plan your communication by using a real-life upcoming presentation.

A dynamic and powerful presentation gives you a platform to communicate your message effectively, influence your audience and spark desired action. Effective presenters spend a considerable amount of time preparing for their presentation, ensuring that the structure, content and communication style is appropriate for their audience. It is often what happens before the presenter gives their presentation that dictates the success of the presentation.

Persuasive Presentation Skills includes the **Persuasive Presentation Skills Presentation Planner**, provided as a free downloadable tool.

Now let's get started!

1	Learning Short-take® > Start here
2	Learning Journal 75
3	Skill Development Action Plan 81
4	Quick Reference 87
5	Next Steps 103

"I use many props. The props act as cue cards reminding me of what to say next."

TOM OGDEN

"*Ask yourself, If I had only sixty seconds on the stage, what would I absolutely have to say to get my message across.*"

JEFF DEWAR

Section 1

LEARNING SHORT-TAKE®

WHAT'S IN THIS LEARNING SHORT-TAKE®

Table of Contents

How to Complete Your Learning Short-take®	5
Activity Checklist	6
Learning Objectives	7
Let's Get Started	8
Part 1 - Getting Started	9
Creating Effective Presentations	10
Types of Presentations	15
From Presentation Start to End - Overview for Success	23
Part 2 - Planning Your Presentation	29
Step 1: Know Your Audience	32
Step 2: Set Clear Objectives	37
Step 3: Create Content Overview & Gather Content	40
Step 4: Create Content Detail & Visual Aids	43
Step 5: Rehearse - Use The Presentation Planner	50
Step 6: Consider Co/Multi-Presenters	55
Step 7: Review	59
Part 3 - The Presentation Day	61
Reducing Nervousness	62
Top Tips for Venue and 'Room' Control	63
Top Tips for Delivering Your Presentation	66
After the Presentation	73
In Closing...	74

HOW TO COMPLETE YOUR LEARNING SHORT-TAKE®

1. **Reflect on your skills and abilities** in preparing for a presentation, and how these skills determine the level of presentation success.

2. **Complete the Activities.**

3. Highlight specific skill areas that you believe you could develop more. Add these to the **Learning Journal.** Add to your Learning Journal as you go.

4. When you have completed this Learning Short-take® **meet with your Manager/Coach.** In this meeting, you will jointly establish a personal **Skill Development Action Plan.**

5. **Subject to your coach's final review** and assessment, you will either sign off the module, or undertake further skill development as appropriate.

"If you wouldn't write it and sign it, don't say it."

EARL WILSON

ACTIVITY CHECKLIST

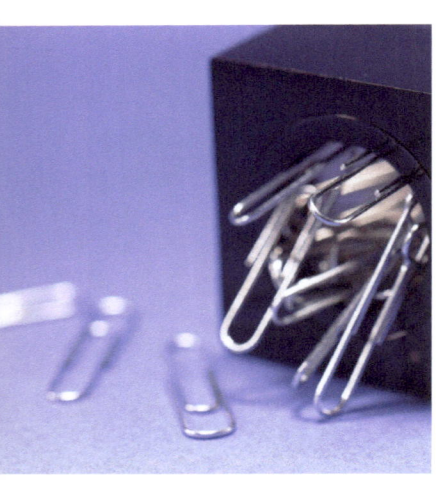

During this Learning Short-take® you will be prompted to complete the following activities:

- Activity # 1 - Initial Skills Self-Assessment 13
- Activity # 2 - Terms and Definitions Match 21
- Activity # 3 - From Deadly Mistakes to Presentation Greats 28
- Activity # 4 - What's Your Story? 48
- Activity # 5 - Presentation Language 53
- Activity # 6 - My Top Tips 72
- Learning Journal 75
- Skill Development Action Plan 81

LEARNING OBJECTIVES

After you have completed this Learning Short-take®, you should be able to:

- Define the importance of preparation in delivering a successful presentation.
- Know how to structure your presentation to deliver key messages.
- Recognize how to connect with your audience and maintain attention.
- Identify key factors for enhancing your message and projecting credibility.
- Design and use visual aids to support your message.
- Describe how to control your nervous energy.
- Create a Skill Development Action Plan.

"Make thyself a craftsman in speech, for thereby though shalt gain the upper hand."

INSCRIPTION FOUND IN A 3,000-YEAR-OLD EGYPTIAN TOMB

LET'S GET STARTED

The power and opportunity we are given every time we present is enormous, yet many presenters have no idea of their potential to influence. A dynamic presentation gives you a platform to communicate your message effectively, influence your audience and spark desired action.

Effective presenters use the energy of their audience to deliver lively and memorable presentations. They also spend a considerable amount of time preparing for their presentation, ensuring that the structure, content and communication style is appropriate for their listeners. It is what happens before the presenter enters the 'room' that dictates the success of the presentation.

This Learning Short-take® combines self-study with workplace activities to provide you with the key skills and techniques to deliver dynamic presentations. Assess your current approach to delivering presentations and develop unique and innovative strategies to improve your level of success. You will work on a real-life presentation opportunity to effectively plan your communication. The Learning Short-take® is designed for completion in approximately 90 minutes. While completing this Learning Short-take® you will prepare your own up-coming presentation to improve your presentation skills.

GETTING STARTED

PART 1

CREATING EFFECTIVE PRESENTATIONS

Today's business environment calls for a variety of presentation types including convention speeches, keynote addresses, reports to board of directors, communication at a team meeting, delivering good and bad news, or communicating organizational change. The goal of the presentation and the aim of the presenter may differ with each of these occasions. However, whether your aim is to motivate, enthrall, entice, deliver facts, provide data, or influence behavior change, solid presentation skills are essential for communication success.

The ability to present professionally is a very useful skill in business, sales, training, public speaking and self-development. In addition to solid presentation techniques, confidence and experience are critical skills in determining the success or failure of a presentation. However, you are not alone if the thought of speaking in public terrifies you. Presenting and public speaking regularly tops the list in surveys of our greatest fears - more than heights, flying or dying.

He started his presentation very nervously and had his head down looking at his script the whole time. We all knew he was nervous. His voice was shaking and at one time he used the laser pointer on a slide and his hands were shaking. His voice was monotone and he mumbled from the beginning to end. He had way too many slides - there must have been 100 of them.
Each slide was just his script retyped into bullet points which he read one by one. After the first 10 minutes of his 90 minute presentation people were checking their phones for messages, leaving the room, doing other tasks and overall no one was listening to a thing. I was hoping that something would change during the presentation to make it better but it didn't. It was painful for us as an audience but clearly more painful and humiliating for the presenter. I felt sorry for him.

This type of presenter is not uncommon, and his symptoms are not unusual. Many people faced with the prospect of public speaking experience a similar physical reaction, which is simply a release of adrenalin into the system. However, the force of this adrenalin is equivalent to drinking seven cups of coffee and results in the nervous feeling of 'butterflies'. Even the most seasoned presenters feel some form of nervousness. It's absolutely normal and a great presenter uses this adrenalin for even greater success. Don't try to eliminate your butterflies - just get them flying in formation.

Preparation = confidence = more relaxed

Good preparation is the key to confidence, which is the key to being relaxed. Good preparation and rehearsal reduces your nerves, decreases the likelihood of errors and communicates to your audience that they are important. Preparation and knowledge are the pre-requisites for a successful presentation, and confidence and control will flow from good preparation. Remember and apply Eleanor Roosevelt's maxim that "no-one can intimidate me without my permission".

A great presentation does not just happen. It is planned, rehearsed then delivered with flair. A good presenter is one who learns the skills of presenting – not one who hopes for talent to carry them through. Public speaking is a skill not a talent. You can be a good presenter if you learn the skills for presentation success. You will be a great speaker if you learn from every presentation you deliver.

We can all learn from the great speakers of the world. Who are the public speakers you admire? Ask yourself why you admire them. What techniques do they use in their speeches that you can use? What principles can you adapt to your presentations? It could be a great political leader, business executive or innovator. Whether it is a Churchill, Henry Ford or Einstein - ask yourself, "Why does their delivery work so well? How can I use that technique or principle in my speech?"

 **Complete Activity # 1**
Initial Skills Self-Assessment

ACTIVITY 1: INITIAL SKILLS SELF-ASSESSMENT

Rate yourself on each of the techniques.
7 is competent and confident, little need for improvement
4 is average, needs improvement
1 is uncomfortable, major need for improvement

- Note specific areas of improvement related to each skill that you would like to develop. Be sure to include your ***reasons*** for your rating in each skill.
- Start thinking about a personal development plan and identify two or three things you could do to improve your skills in this area and write them in the space provided.

I…	Rating	Reasoning
include as many relevant facts and research data as I can to persuade my audience and let the facts speak for themselves.	1 2 3 4 5 6 7	
begin my presentations with a greeting such as "Thank you for having me," "Good Morning," "It's nice to be here" or "Ladies and gentlemen."	1 2 3 4 5 6 7	
almost always use PowerPoint in my formal presentations.	1 2 3 4 5 6 7	
use different words and a different mannerism when I am at a relaxed dinner party with friends than I do when I am giving a formal business presentation.	1 2 3 4 5 6 7	
focus on delivering intelligent and thoughtful presentations rather than presentations which are humorous and entertaining.	1 2 3 4 5 6 7	
structure my presentations into parts and within each part I delve into specifics.	1 2 3 4 5 6 7	
avoid gimmicks and concentrate on the matter at hand - conveying the concepts as clearly as possible.	1 2 3 4 5 6 7	
believe that people should remember the information I present, rather than the way I present.	1 2 3 4 5 6 7	
present visuals that combine text, numbers and suitable business graphics.	1 2 3 4 5 6 7	

ACTIVITY 1: CONTINUED

I…	Rating	Reasoning
tend to be more factual than speculative in my presentations.	1 2 3 4 5 6 7	
rely on experience, research and case studies to drive my point home.	1 2 3 4 5 6 7	
use relevant personal and business stories, analogies and metaphors to help explain difficult data or new concepts.	1 2 3 4 5 6 7	

Personal development plan ideas:

1

2

Now update your Learning Journal (page 75)

TYPES OF PRESENTATIONS

The following is an overview of several common types of presentations and their purpose.

Informative Presentations

The purpose of an informative presentation is to **communicate information, facts and data**. Keep an informative presentation brief and to the point. Stick to the facts and avoid complicated information. Use one or a combination of the following structures to communicate this information.

Chronological Structure

- Explains when things should happen.
- Works best with visual people or people who can see the overall organization or sequence of events.
- Use words like "first," "second," "third," to list order.

Location Structure

- Explains where things should happen.
- Works best with people who understand the group or area you are talking about.
- Use words like "Region 1, 2, 3, or 4" to explain order.

Cause and Effect Structure

- Explains how things should happen.
- Works best with people who understand the relationship between events.
- Use phrases like "Because of _____, we now have to _____".
- Simply list items in their order of importance.

"Of those who say nothing, few are silent."

THOMAS NEIEL

Instructional Presentations

The purpose of an instructional presentation is to **give specific directions or orders**. Your presentation will probably be slightly longer, given that it has to cover your topic in detail. In an instructional presentation, your listeners should come away with new knowledge or a new skill.

- Explain why the information or skill is valuable to the audience.
- Explain the learning objectives of the instructional program.
- Demonstrate the process.
- Provide participants the opportunity to ask questions, give, and receive feedback from you and their peers.
- Connect the learning to actual use.
- Have participants state how they will use it.

Attention Grabbing Presentations

The purpose of an attention grabbing presentation is to **make people think about a certain problem or situation**. You want to arouse the audience's emotions and intellect so that they will be receptive to your point of view. Use vivid language in an attention grabbing presentation to project sincerity and enthusiasm.

- Gain attention with a story that illustrates (and sometimes exaggerates) the problem.
- Show the need to solve the problem and illustrate it with an example that is general or commonplace.
- Describe your solution for a satisfactory resolution to the problem.
- Compare/contrast the two worlds with the problem solved and unsolved.
- Call the audience to action to help solve the problem.
- Give the audience a directive that is clear, easy, and immediate.

"The older I grow the more I listen to people who don't talk much."

GERMAIN G. GLIEN

Persuasive Presentations

The purpose of a persuasive presentation is to **convince your listeners to accept your proposal**. A convincing persuasive presentation offers a solution to a controversy, dispute, or problem. To succeed with a persuasive presentation, you must present sufficient logic, evidence, and emotion to sway the audience to your viewpoint.

- Create a great introduction. A persuasive presentation introduction must accomplish the following:
    - Seize the audience's attention.
    - Disclose the problem or needs that your product or service will satisfy.
    - Tantalize the audience by describing the advantages of solving the problem or need.
- Create a desire for the audience to agree with you by describing exactly how your product or service will satisfy their needs.
- Close your persuasive presentation with a call to action.
    - Ask for the decision that you want to be made.
    - Ask for the course of action that you want to be followed.

Decision-Making Presentations

The purpose of a decision-making presentation is to **move your audience to take your suggested action**. A decision-making presentation presents ideas, suggestions, and arguments strongly enough to persuade an audience to carry out your requests.

In a decision-making presentation, you must tell the audience what to do and how to do it. You should also let them know what will happen if they don't do what you ask.

- Gain attention with a story that illustrates the problem.
- Show the need to solve the problem and illustrate it with an example that is general or commonplace.
- Describe your solution to bring a satisfactory resolution to the problem.
- Compare/contrast the two worlds with the problem solved and unsolved.
- Call the audience to action to help solve the problem and give them a way to be part of the solution.

Communicating Bad News

No one wants to be the bearer of bad news, however there are things you can do to soften the blow. The next time you have to present less-than-favourable information, keep the following tips in mind.

Tailor your presentation appropriately

Don't use bright colors, cartoons, sound-effects or zany fonts if your PowerPoint presentation contains a series of grim statistics. Stick to a simple background color (or use a standard corporate template) and clear sans-serif font. Save transitions and animation effects for a more upbeat presentation.

Don't invite extra spectators

When you schedule a bad-news meeting, it's particularly important to invite only those people necessary to the discussion.

Include a positive spin

Bad news is always easier to take if it's delivered with a positive spin. For example, if you must report that the results of your company's latest advertising strategy are less than favorable, you'll also want to include some positive news. After you've reviewed the key results of your research, conclude with a recommendations section. If consumers hated the look of the ad, but thought the copy was well written, recommend that future advertising use the same copy direction but a different layout.

Don't 'sugarcoat' it

On the other hand, be careful not to 'sugarcoat' the information. You have an obligation to share the facts, even if they're alarming or upsetting to others within the organization. After all, it's business. Numbers fall, campaigns fail, employees don't work out, and the economy slumps. People cope with bad news every day. Be forthright, objective and optimistic. It's the best way to deliver bad news.

Complete Activity # 2
Terms & Definitions Match

ACTIVITY 2: TERMS AND DEFINITIONS MATCH

Draw a line linking the term in the left column, with the correct definition in the right column.

Bad News Presentations	The purpose of this presentation is to communicate information, facts and data. Stick to the facts and avoid complicated information.
Decision-Making Presentations	The purpose of this presentation is to give specific directions or orders. Listeners should come away with new knowledge or a new skill.
Persuasive Presentations	The purpose of this presentation is to make people think about a certain problem or situation. You want to arouse the audience's emotions and intellect so that they will be receptive to your point of view.
Informative Presentations	The purpose of this presentation is to convince your listeners to accept your proposal. You must present sufficient logic, evidence, and emotion to sway the audience to your viewpoint.
Attention Grabbing Presentations	The purpose of this presentation is to move your audience to take your suggested action. You must tell the audience what to do and how to do it. You should also let them know what will happen if they don't do what you ask.
Instructional Presentations	The purpose of this presentation is to deliver unfavorable information.

Activity # 2 – Check your Answers

Check your work from the previous activity.

Terms	Definitions
Informative Presentations	The purpose of this presentation is to communicate information, facts and data. Stick to the facts and avoid complicated information.
Instructional Presentations	The purpose of this presentation is to give specific directions or orders. Listeners should come away with new knowledge or a new skill.
Attention Grabbing Presentations	The purpose of this presentation is to make people think about a certain problem or situation. You want to arouse the audience's emotions and intellect so that they will be receptive to your point of view.
Persuasive Presentations	The purpose of this presentation is to convince your listeners to accept your proposal. You must present sufficient logic, evidence, and emotion to sway the audience to your viewpoint.
Decision-Making Presentations	The purpose of this presentation is to move your audience to take your suggested action. You must tell the audience what to do and how to do it. You should also let them know what will happen if they don't do what you ask.
Bad News Presentations	The purpose of this presentation is to deliver unfavorable information.

Now update your Learning Journal (page 75)

FROM PRESENTATION START TO END - OVERVIEW FOR SUCCESS

Creating Impact – The Presentation Start

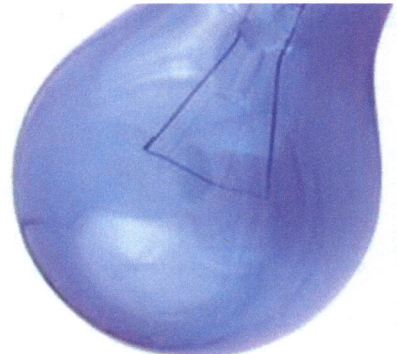

- Generally, you have 4 - 7 seconds in which to make a positive impact and good opening impression, so make sure you have a good, strong, solid introduction, and rehearse it to death. Try to build your own credibility and create a safe comfortable environment for your audience. Smiling helps.

- Don't start with a joke unless you are supremely confident that you can 'pull it off'. Jokes are a high risk strategy at the best of times, let alone at the start of a presentation.

- Don't apologize for anything up-front unless you have made a serious error. This will be perceived as a lack of confidence and a sign of weakness by your audience.

- Try to start on time even if some of the audience is late.

- The average attention span of an average adult listener is only 6 - 8 minutes, so present your material using a variety of stimuli, media and movement to maintain maximum interest.

Adding interest throughout the presentation

- Memorize or build into your visuals a couple of good quotes and always credit the source. Having quotes and other devices is important to give your presentation depth and texture, as well as keeping your audience interested.

"If the only tool in your toolbox is a hammer you'll treat everything as a nail." (Abraham Maslow)

- Be daring and bold and include a level of entertainment in your presentation that is appropriate for your audience. The more senses you can stimulate the more fun your audience will have and the more they'll remember.
    - Create opportunities to take notes, via handouts and other items that you can distribute.
    - If presenting virtually, distribute handouts/items in advance. If this is not possible, ask an associate to help you and build in time for distribution during the presentation.
    - Create analogies and themes, and use props to illustrate and reinforce them.

- Examples of interest that you can use to bring your presentation to life, and keep your audience attentive and enjoying themselves:

  - Stories
  - Questions
  - Pictures, cartoons and video-clips
  - Sound-clips
  - Straw polls
  - Audience participation exercises
  - Quotations
  - Props
  - Examples
  - Analogies
- Statistics (which dramatically improve audience 'buy-in' if you're trying to persuade)
- Your body language
- Changing tone and pitch of your voice.

Managing Longer Presentations

- For longer presentations, if you're not an experienced speaker, you must schedule a break every 45 minutes or so for people to get up and stretch their legs, otherwise you'll be losing them regardless of the amount of interest you include.

- Take the pressure off yourself by not speaking all the time. Get the audience doing things, and make use of all the communications senses available.

Creating Impact - The Presentation Close

- Prepare a memorable close. Quotes, a personal or professional story, a concise summary are all examples of ways of ending your presentation with impact.

- To ensure the audience knows its 'the end', simply saying "Thank you" or "I'd like to conclude with…"

- If the audience applauds stop and silently acknowledge their applause before leaving the podium. Remembering to smile will leave your audience with the memory of a great presenter.

Seven Deadly Presentation Mistakes

1. Apologizing in advance.
2. Failing to explain the reasons why the subject has any relevance or value to the audience.
3. Using a presentation designed for one audience – for a different audience.
4. Telling the audience more than they want to know.
5. Showing detailed or irrelevant slides, or only 1-2 very static slides whilst reading a script
6. Reading verbatim every word on every visual.
7. Failing to rehearse – "it'll be OK on the day!"

Complete Activity # 3
From Deadly Mistakes to Presentation Greats

ACTIVITY 3: FROM DEADLY MISTAKES TO PRESENTATION GREATS

For each of the seven deadly mistakes listed below, develop strategies to turn these mistakes into great presentation techniques.

Deadly Mistake	How I could make this 'deadly mistake' a 'presentation great'
Apologizing in advance.	
Failing to explain the reasons why the subject has any relevance or value to the audience.	
Using a presentation designed for one audience – for a different audience.	
Telling the audience more than they want to know.	
Showing detailed or irrelevant slides, or only 1-2 very static slides whilst reading a script.	
Reading verbatim every word on every visual.	
Failing to rehearse – "it'll be OK on the day!"	

Now update your Learning Journal (page 75)

PLANNING YOUR PRESENTATION

PART 2

PLANNING YOUR PRESENTATION

Successful presentations are planned and rehearsed well in advance of the event. Even the most skilled presenters rarely 'wing it' and what may appear to be an 'off the cuff' presentation is probably a well thought out and structured approach.

The following 7-step process will assist you to prepare for your presentation from beginning to end. Regardless of the nature of your presentation, this structured approach will keep you on track for success.

The steps of the Presentation Planning are as follows:

1) Know Your Audience
2) Set a Clear Objective
3) Create Content Overview & Gather Content
4) Develop Content Detail & Create Visual Aids
5) Rehearse
6) Consider Co-/Multi Presenters
7) Evaluate your Presentation

PRESENTATION PLANNER

Within this Learning Short-take® is The Presentation Planner. This tool will assist you in creating presentations. Download it now. You will use The Presentation Planner to prepare for an up-coming real life presentation.

FREE DOWNLOAD

To download this tool go to https://www.catherinemattiske.com/books and follow the online instructions.

STEP 1: KNOW YOUR AUDIENCE

When you have a presentation to make, it's human nature to jump straight into 'content mode', asking yourself, "What am I going to say? How much information can I fit into the allotted time? Which visuals should I use?" As a result you may find yourself rushing prematurely into the process of selecting material, developing an outline, creating slides and rehearsing content.

Although these steps are important, you risk heading off in the wrong direction unless you first consider your audience. Your audience is in fact, the most important aspect of your presentation.

As an effective presenter, your first step toward making a powerful, persuasive presentation is to define your audience. Who are your listeners and what are their needs? To begin your preparation without this information could result in a significant waste of time and effort for both you and your audience.

By defining your audience, you lay the foundation for a successful presentation, increase the likelihood of influencing audience behavior and get the results you want.

Benefits of Defining Your Audience

As a result of defining your audience, you are able to:

- Identify what motivates your listeners to act.
- Tailor your content to give them specifically what they want, need and expect.
- Project an appropriate presentation style and personality.
- Increase your comfort level as a speaker.
- Obtain your objective for making the presentation.

Defining your audience means finding out who they are. This information is critical in addressing audience needs, interests, expectations and levels of understanding. Without this knowledge, you are unable to match your message with their needs. Your ability to present from *their* perspective enables you to influence their thinking, persuade them to accept what you are suggesting and achieve your presentation objectives.

Audience analysis is collecting and reviewing information about the people who will be the recipients of your presentation. You should routinely analyze who the audience is and what they want to accomplish by listening to your presentation. You need this kind of information to ensure that you're designing and writing your presentation for your audience.

ARISTOTLE GAVE SOME ADVICE IN 380 B.C. WHICH STILL HOLDS TODAY:

"The fool persuades me with his reasons;
the wise man persuades me with my own."

Having an understanding of your audience will allow your message to be pitched at the correct level. Not having this understanding may result in a presentation that is disconnected to the audience either by way of presentation style or the level of content being presented.

By defining your audience members and tailoring your message to specifically address their reasons, wants and needs, you are able to deliver a presentation that engages, informs and persuades. By having an understanding of your audience and customizing your presentation to meet their needs they are most likely to give you their time and attention.

Consider the following techniques and choose the appropriate ways for you to collect information regarding your audience:

- Speak to the participants days or weeks before the presentation.
- Send out a questionnaire or survey to audience members.
- Speak to their co-workers or managers.
- Research audience-related issues and gather current data on their industry.
- Converse and mingle with participants at an event prior to your presentation or directly before the presentation itself.
- Ask questions during the presentation to gather on-the-spot feedback.
- Talk to the participants after the presentation to verify that your intended message was received and their needs met.
- Ask audience members to complete an evaluation and give feedback after your presentation.

The Presentation Planner contains an Audience Assessment Checklist which includes audience considerations for preparing for a successful presentation. Completing this step will help ensure that the material you're developing will suit the needs, interests, and abilities of your audience. The Audience Assessment Checklist will allow you to identify what you know about your audience and what you'll need to find out.

Download the **The Presentation Planner** from https://www.catherinemattiske.com/books

Activity using The Presentation Planner - Analyze Audience

Complete **only** the following sections of The Presentation Planner...

- Presentation Information
- 1 - Audience Assessment Checklist

You will create the remaining parts of The Presentation Planner later.

STEP 2: SET CLEAR OBJECTIVES

What is the message you want to convey? What are your objectives in talking to your audience? What knowledge or experience do you have that can benefit people?

An effective presentation demands that you market your topic and yourself. You have to sell your ideas and yourself to the audience. Regardless of the size of the audience, whether internal or external, you are still selling a message.

A presentation will have at least one of four aims: to inform, to entertain, to touch the emotions, or to move to action. Successful presentations will likely include all four aims.

Writing clear objectives

The Aim is a short sentence that starts with an action verb and defines what you want to accomplish in the presentation.

Objectives describe the specific actions that you want to occur either during or as a result of your meeting or presentation.

- What *specific desired outcomes* do I personally want from this event?
- What action do I want *my audience* to take as a result of my presentation?
- What must audience members know, say or do differently when they leave my presentation?
- When are these actions required?

SAMPLE – Presenting at a Meeting

Meeting Aim: Develop Plan for New Employee Recruitment

Objectives in order to achieve the objective:
- Identify new College Graduate Personnel hiring needs
- Discuss/confirm colleges and universities targeted for on-campus recruiting
  - Understand last year's results
  - Suggest/agree adds and deletes
- Specify materials needed for advance solicitation of candidates
- Identify/assign on-campus recruiters
- Outline work plans and agree who does what by when

SAMPLE – Presenting to a Larger Group

Presentation Aim: Jump-start Quarterly Sales Campaign

Objectives in order to achieve the objective:
- Review and celebrate successes within year-to-date sales results
- Identify product lines and customer groups with below-objective year-to-date purchases and specify actions needed
- Review marketing support for the quarter
- Answer questions and listen to "what's on your mind"
- Present "Sales Tip of the Quarter"
- Discuss and get buy-in on sales objectives for the quarter
- Recognize high-achievers

Continue in your downloaded Presentation Planner from https://www.catherinemattiske.com/books

Activity using The Presentation Planner - Set Objectives

Complete **only** the following sections of The Presentation Planner…

- 2 - Set Clear Objectives

You will create the remaining parts of The Presentation Planner later.

STEP 3: CREATE CONTENT OVERVIEW & GATHER CONTENT

Using **The Presentation Planner** the next step of planning for your presentation is to create a high level agenda and then collect all of the content you need to present.

Questions to ask yourself during this part of the planning are 'why', 'what' and 'why not'. The content of your presentation will form the 'what', i.e. what are you presenting? Its important to solidify your thoughts on what you want to accomplish in your presentation. Developing an agenda will create a efficient and effective guide for your presentation.

1 - Content Overview - The Agenda

What Key Points or Recommendations must your presentation include to support or develop your main strategy and persuade your audience?

Using Post-It Notes™ brainstorm the main content areas of your presentation. Write one idea per Post-It Note™. Brainstorming is all about quantity, not quality, so ensure that all of your ideas are recorded.

Once all of your ideas are recorded begin to cluster similar ideas into logical groups. These will become your topics.

2 - Content Details - Gathering the Content

1) Using the Presentation Planner, write each topic heading and consider how you will gather the information.
2) For each topic create a list of sub-topics.
3) Summarize all resources you need to research the topic.
4) List the jargon that you'll need to define or avoid. This will help guide you when writing each part of your presentation.

A visual representation of the Presentation Flow

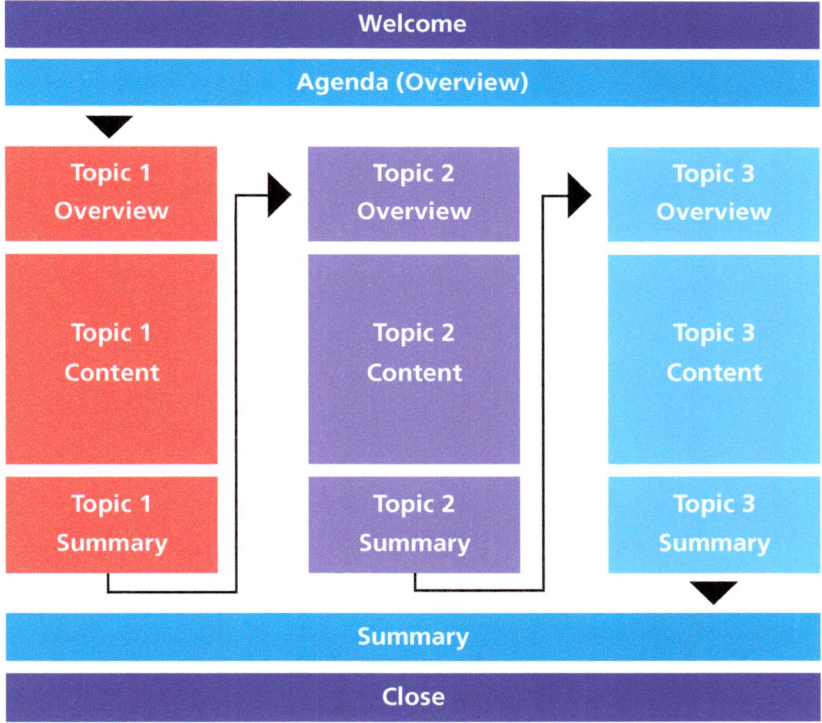

Continue in your downloaded **Presentation Planner** from https://www.catherinemattiske.com/books

Activity using The Presentation Planner - Create Content Overview & Gather Content

Complete **only** the following sections of The Presentation Planner...

- 3 - Create Content Overview & Gather Content

You will create the remaining parts of The Presentation Planner later.

STEP 4: CREATE CONTENT DETAIL & VISUAL AIDS

When creating a presentation the following must be completed:

- Consider Visuals
- Write Presentation
    - Introduction
    - Topics
    - Prepare for Questions
    - Presentation Close
- Logistics and Supporting Materials

Using Visual Aids Why Bother With Visuals?

We learn through our senses. Presentations generally use both hearing and sight. These visual aids are an essential way to increase retention of your message.

Visual Aids are especially important if you are presenting virtually.

1.0%	taste
1.5%	touch
3.5%	smell
11.0%	hearing
83.0%	sight

Using Visual Aids for Impact and Message Retention

- Printed visual aids with several paragraphs of text, should be designed using serif fonts (typeface) for quicker readability. Arial is a sans serif font. Times New Roman is a serif font. (A serif font is one with the extra little cross-lines which finish off the strokes of the letters. Interestingly, serif fonts originated in the days of engraving, before printing, when the engraver needed an exit point from each letter.)

- Extensive sections of text can be read more quickly in serif font because the words have a horizontal flow, but serif fonts have a more old-fashioned traditional appearance than sans serif. If you need to comply with a company type-style you may not have a choice. **Whatever the situation, try to select fonts and point sizes that are fit for the medium and purpose.**

- Use no more than two different fonts and no more than two font variants (size/bold/italic), otherwise your presentation will become confusing. If in doubt simply pick a good readable serif font and use it big and bold for headings, and 14 - 16 point size for the body text.

- Absolutely avoid upper case (capital letters) in body text, because your audience needs to be able to read word-shapes as well as the letters. Upper case makes every word a rectangle, so it takes a long time to read. Upper case may be appropriate for a heading if you feel that it is really necessary.

- Create your own prompts and notes to suit your presentation flow and your level of confidence. Cue cards can be useful, however you need to ensure that they are numbered or held together in order. A simple running sheet (summary flow) that you can quickly glance at is a great safety-net for anything longer than half and hour. You can use this to monitor your timing and pace.

Designing and Preparing Visual Material

Combining the visual with the verbal gives tremendous strength to any communication and is much more effective than when either is used alone. However. regardless of the amount time, effort and money you spend on visual aids, they can never prop up a poorly prepared presentation. Using visual aids doesn't ensure a successful presentation. If a visual aid doesn't help get your message across, don't use it. A good presentation without visual aids is better than a poor visual aid demonstration.

Be Selective	Determine if visual aids are necessary, then assess whether a simple aid like a flipchart, digital whiteboard or summary handout is enough. If necessary, investigate other visual possibilities.
Ensure Relevance	Does it help your subject matter, or does it detract from it? Does it contain information that you will not be discussing? Is it appropriate for the level of knowledge of your audience? Will it provoke unwanted questions?
Don't Overdo It	The characteristics of a good visual are closely allied to the standard principles of an effective presentation.
Be Accurate	Provide a correct interpretation of the facts.
Be Clear	Keep it neat, bold and clearly readable by all. Translate unfamiliar terms and concepts so that people understand them. If you have an above average knowledge of your subject it is easy to overcomplicate your message.
Be Simple	Keep it short and to the point.
Be Direct	Focus sharply on the main idea you must get across.
Be the Right Size	Visual aids must be large enough to be seen by everyone. If presenting in a room >24pt is recommended.
Be Colorful	Use color wisely. Don't be too lavish. It is better to have too few colors than too many. Use red in moderation and avoid yellow unless in a highlighting capacity.
Be Imaginative	You don't have to be an artist. Remember the purpose of your visual and don't over-clutter it. There are plenty of visual design packages, infographics and templates available.

Continue in your downloaded **Presentation Planner** from https://www.catherinemattiske.com/books

Activity using The Presentation Planner - Create Content Detail & Visual Aids

Complete **only** the following sections of The Presentation Planner…

- 4 – Create Content Detail & Visual Aids
    - Consider Visuals
    - Introduction
    - Topics
        - Use the structure on the Presentation Planner for each of your topics (use extra pages as required)
    - Prepare for Questions
    - Presentation Close
    - Logistics and Supporting Materials

You will create the remaining parts of The Presentation Planner later.

Adding Impact: Telling Stories

Tell stories to give your presentation impact and call your audience to action. Paint word pictures that create images in the listeners' minds. If they can see it they are more likely to understand and remember your message. The best public speakers are storytellers. Use stories and anecdotes to illustrate and reinforce the main points of your presentation.

The best stories are personal. When they are your own they are easier to remember and make your presentation unique. We listen to stories. Generally we dislike long lectures. If you have forgotten that lesson - just ask a child. The way to find personal stories that can be used in your presentations is to write them down. Make a list of significant things that have happened to you and those around you; the first time you did something, your best times, worst times, the biggest mistake, the best break, the greatest 'ah-ha', the funniest moment, the most frustrating incident, the dumbest thing you did, the most embarrassing moment etc.

The things that drive you the most make the best stories to tell in your presentations. Rehearse your stories and edit them down into a short narrative that is easy to listen to. While it may be hard for you to leave out some of the details, it will be harder for your audience to listen to unnecessary information. The key to success is keeping it short, sharp and relevant.

Complete Activity # 4
What's Your Story?

ACTIVITY 4: WHAT'S YOUR STORY?

Consider your upcoming presentation. Research an appropriate story that fits with your content, or develop your own.

Record your story in the space provided below.

Now update your Learning Journal (page 75)

Handling Q&A Sessions

You can better prepare for questions following your presentation if you spend some time pre-empting audience reactions. This is time well invested and will help raise your credibility and professionalism in the eyes of your audience. Suggestions for managing your question and answer session include:

- Having several statements ready. Use your answers to emphasise the main points you want to drive home.
- Accepting questions from the entire audience. Most speakers tend to favour the right or left side of the room, or in a virtual presentation only who they can see on-screen. Be careful not to focus on a particular segment.
- Listening intently to questions. Repeat each one in your head and recite it (if it's positive) back to the questioner.
- Rephrasing negative questions. You can recast embarrassing questions by wording them differently. For example, if someone asks why your firm is 'polluting the environment', you can say, 'the question was about the environment and what we're doing about it'.
- Addressing the entire audience. Look first at the person who asked the question, then engage everyone with eye contact.
- Being brief. Get to the point quickly. Remember: the audience has already sat through your presentation.
- If you don't know, say so. Contact the person a day or so later with the answer. Word will spread.
- Setting a limit on the questions. It helps to arrange a wrap-up signal with your host.
- Making your responses credible. Quote reliable outside experts. Round off statistics and other numbers to make them easy to remember. Give references to your own experience such as 'in my 15 years as a …'
- Learning to bridge. You can return to your main points by saying 'that's important, I think the main issue is …'

STEP 5: REHEARSE - USE THE PRESENTATION PLANNER

Remembering your speech

'The best public speakers do not memorize their presentation'. Know the topic and the issues, and then make notes for yourself. Avoid reading your presentation or you are at risk of boring your audience.

Instead write key words that remind you of the important communication messages. Ensure your notes are easy for you to follow and that you can read them comfortably from a distance.

Rehearsing your presentation

Rehearse your presentation on your feet at least three times. It feels different when you speak standing up. Get used to the feel of delivering your presentation and this will maximize your success on the day. You can also practice important parts of your presentation while sitting in your car or at your desk.

Editing For The Ear

Unlike the reader, the listener cannot pause to reconsider a phrase or paragraph that didn't connect with them the first time through. The listener has to move right along with the speaker or risk losing even more of the presentation. In the time he or she spends reconsidering one point, two or three others may be lost. This gives the speaker a special responsibility in keeping the audience with them from the beginning of a presentation to the end.

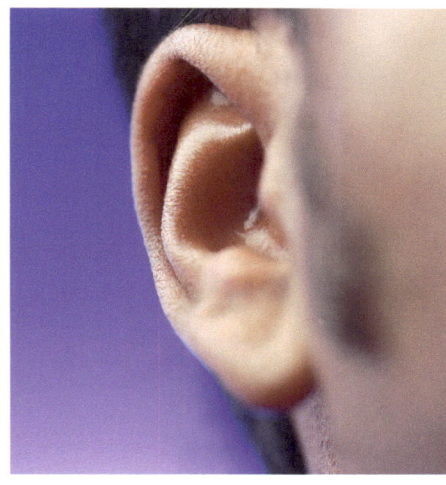

1. **Aim for simplicity.** (Never use a long word when a short one works; use simple sentences.)
2. **Use the active voice rather than the passive voice whenever possible.** (Say "Marketing prepared the report", not "The report was prepared by Marketing.")
3. **Be Politically Correct.** Guard against using words that could turn off or offend the audience.
4. **Vary your pattern of speech.** (Guard against using words and phrases repetitively; vary sentence length and structure.)

Continue in your downloaded **Presentation Planner** from https://www.catherinemattiske.com/books

Activity using The Presentation Planner

Complete **only** the following sections of The Presentation Planner…

- 5 - Rehearsal Plan

You will create the remaining parts of The Presentation Planner later.

Complete Activity # 5
Presentation Language

ACTIVITY 5: PRESENTATION LANGUAGE

Replace each of the following words with a simpler one:

Approximately

Cognisant

Disseminate

Endeavour

Numerous

Precipitate

Recapitulate

Remunerate

Subsequent

Some people use words which they think will impress others. Some examples of such words are given below. Replace them with plain English:

Classification device

Macro

Micro

Eventuated

Nomenclature

Parlance

Pursuant to

Unlawful or arbitrary

Deprivation of life

ACTIVITY 5: CONTINUED

The use of foreign words, sexist and racial terms, and jargon can alienate people. Correct the following words or terms.:

Businessmen _____

Fait accompli _____

Mankind _____

Interfaces _____

Manpower _____

Now update your Learning Journal (page 75)

STEP 6: CONSIDER CO/MULTI-PRESENTERS

Working with Team Presentations

Anyone who's ever delivered a team presentation can appreciate the difficulty of synchronizing a group. Team presentations can be a fantastic way to build momentum and interest. They can also be extremely time consuming. If you decide to deliver a group presentation, consider the following strategies to keep audience attention and interest.

Team Leader

A good leader is critical. The Team Leader needs to define the strategy, set the tone and explain the message. If the Team Leader simply delegates a different segment of the presentation to each team member, the result will be a 'mishmash' of styles and tone.

The Team

While technical competence is a crucial component in selecting a team, individual personalities are just as important. Do you have someone who can tell stories and entertain the audience? Do you have someone who's good at moderating in the event that the Q & A session gets out of hand? Do you have someone who can confidently assure audience members if they get skittish? Make sure every person on your team can contribute something to the group.

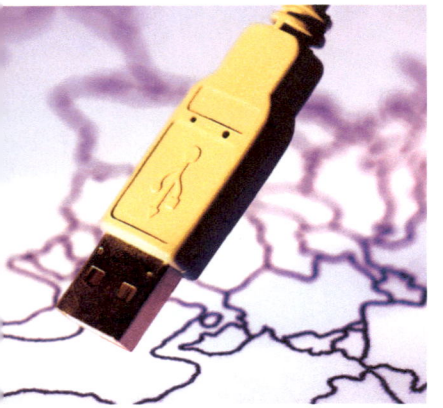

Synchronization

If your preparation time is short, you may want each team member to create their own visual aids. The key is to ensure the format is standardized. The easiest way to do this is to create a master slide in your presentation software and make sure that everyone follows it to the letter. Your master slide should define the background, font, headings and subheadings, text and graphics.

Once all the segments have been completed, assign one member with the task of putting the whole thing together and checking each slide for consistency. While visual consistency ensures a professional-looking presentation, a strong, consistent message will really make your presentation stand out. Make sure everyone is clear on the aim of the presentation, the grammatical style, the acceptable amount of jargon, the level of formality and anything else that will influence the message.

Introduction, Transitions and the Conclusion

As part of your preparation make sure you've assigned one person to do the introductions and that everyone is clear how they're going to make the transition to the next speaker. Once the presentation is over, have one team member wrap up the session and thank the audience for their time.

If presenting virtually, consider who will share and advance the visuals, and how you will communicate and hand over without being able to see each other directly? Book a tech rehearsal!

Handling Questions

Make sure you've defined your core team members' competencies before you go into the presentation. Then, when the Q&A session rolls around, you'll know exactly who should answer which type of questions. It's amazing how many people will attempt to answer questions about which a co-presenter is the expert. Also, keep answers short and to the point. Even though it's your area of expertise, there's no need to deliver a long monologue to the detriment of the overall presentation.

Continue in your downloaded Presentation Planner from https://www.catherinemattiske.com/books

Activity using The Presentation Planner

Complete **only** the following sections of The Presentation Planner…

- 6 - Co/Multi-Presenter Plan

You will create the remaining parts of The Presentation Planner later.

STEP 7: REVIEW

Once your presentation is complete it's very easy to walk off the stage or leave the in-person/virtual meeting room and go on with other tasks. The disciplined presenter learns from his or her presentation and conducts a formal or informal review. Even taking a few minutes to reflect on what went well during your presentation and taking note of what could have worked better will better prepare you for next time you present.

"A theme is a memory aid, it helps you through the presentation just as it also provides the thread of continuity for your audience."

DAVE CAREY

Continue in your downloaded **Presentation Planner** from https://www.catherinemattiske.com/books

Activity using The Presentation Planner

Complete the remaining section of The Presentation Planner…

- 7 - Review

This will finalize your planning.

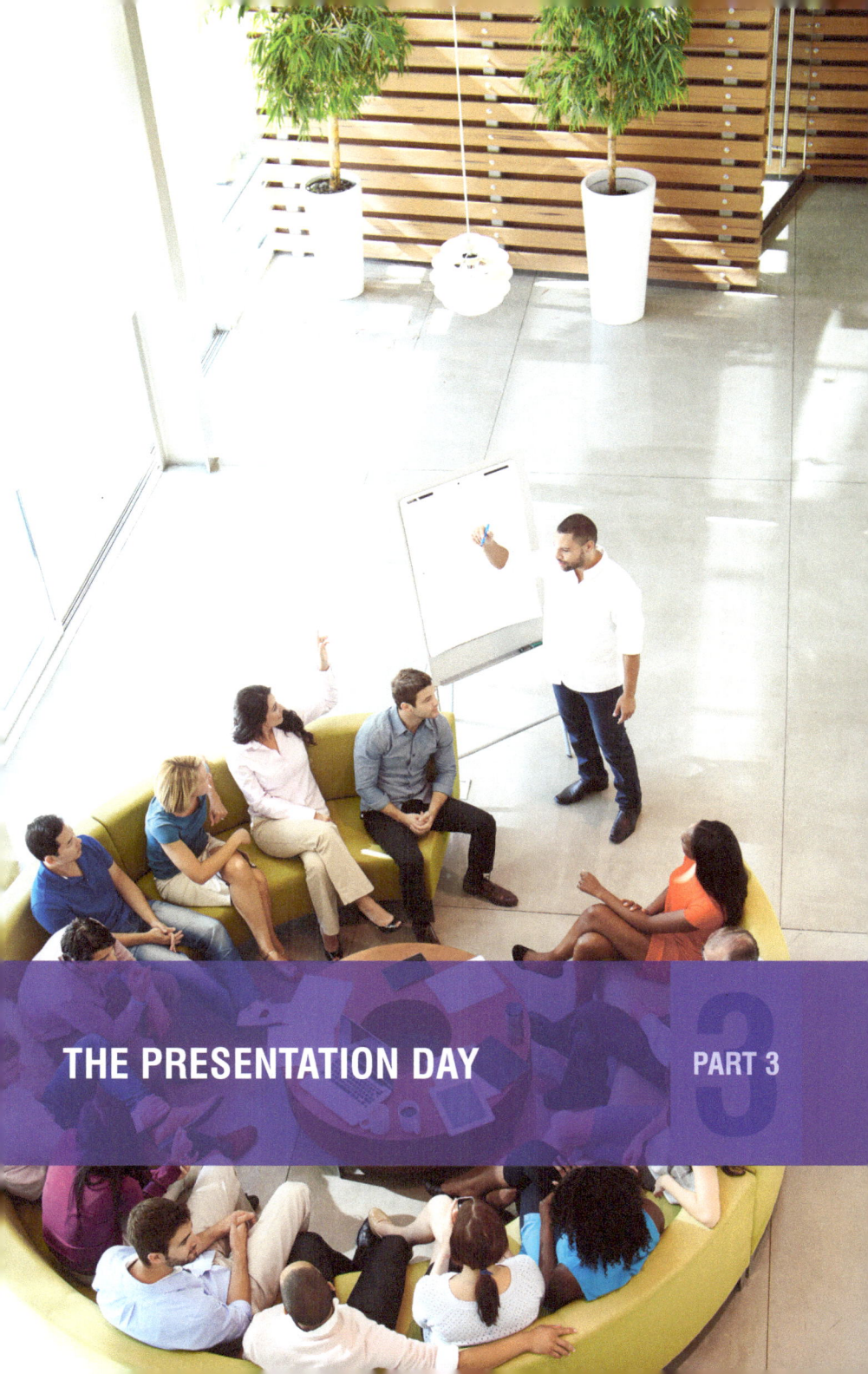

THE PRESENTATION DAY

PART 3

REDUCING NERVOUSNESS

Know the material well (be an expert).	**Accept some fears as being good** (energizing stress vs. destructive).
Practice your presentation (Pilot test, rehearse, and record yourself on video).	**Introduce yourself** to the group in advance (via a social context).
Use **involvement** techniques (audience participation).	**Identify your fears**, categorise them as controllable or uncontrollable, and confront them.
Learn participants' **names** and use them.	Give special emphasis to the **first five minutes** (super-preparation).
Establish your **credibility** early.	**Practice responses** to tough questions or situations.
Use **eye contact** to establish rapport.	**Imagine yourself as a good speaker** (self-fulfilling prophecy).
Exhibit **advance preparation** (via handouts, etc.)	In advance, **check** the facilities (if In-person), software and tech, and check all equipment.
Anticipate potential problems (and **prepare probable responses**).	**Obtain information about the group in advance** (through observation or questionnaire).
Use your **own words** (don't read).	Convince yourself to **relax** (breathe deeply; meditate; talk to yourself).
Put yourself in the audiences' shoes (they're asking, **"What's in it for me?"**)	Prepare an **outline** and follow it.
Assume they are **on your side** (they aren't necessarily antagonistic or hostile).	Get **plenty of rest** so that you are physically and psychologically alert.
Provide an **overview** of the presentation (state the end objectives).	Use your **own style** (don't imitate someone else).

TOP TIPS FOR VENUE AND 'ROOM' CONTROL

Take nothing for granted. Whether your presentation is In-person or virtual, check and double-check, and plan contingencies for anything that might go wrong. Plan and control the layout of the room or your virtual environment as much as you are able. If you are a speaker at someone else's event you'll not have much of a say in this, but if it's your event then take care to position yourself, your equipment and your audience and the seating plan so that it suits you and the situation. For instance, don't lay out a room theatre-style if you want people to participate in teams. Use a boardroom layout if you want a co-operative debating approach.

Make sure everyone can see the visual displays. Make sure you understand and if appropriate control and convey the domestic arrangements (fire drill, catering, messages, breaks etc.).

In-Person Room Setup

Arrange access to the room before your audience arrives to check the setup and get a feel for the layout. This helps to make it your room. Walk around the room and sit in a few different chairs to take in the feel of your room and how your audience will see you.

Virtual Room Setup

Rehearse with and test your virtual meeting setup and software in advance. Explore and select the best on-screen layout and panels display for your needs.

Pre-Presentation Essentials

In advance, complete thorough tech-checks, check your equipment and put on your busiest slide to check for readability. Drink one or two glasses of warm water to both lubricate your vocal cords and hydrate yourself. Be aware that public speaking can dehydrate you.

Emergency exits

Check the exit doors and paths from the building. If an emergency occurs the audience will look to you, the speaker, for leadership and maybe their lives. Be prepared to tell people how to leave the room and building. If it becomes necessary, direct your audience to the exits in a calm, commanding and confident voice. Public speaking carries the responsibility of leadership.

Look your best

Smile. When you smile you look confident and help to improve the confidence of your audience. You will appear more trustworthy, friendly and confident when you smile. Your audience does not want to listen to a speaker who is frowning, or they may automatically prepare for bad news or disengage from the information.

Think through carefully what you will wear on the day. Ensure that you do not wear distracting jewelry and try to keep the color of your clothing blending well with the colors in your slideshow. You are as much a visual aid as your presentation slides. Look in a mirror and check that you look great! You do not need your audience focused on a crooked tie, undone button, smudged make-up, something in your pocket, or anything else that takes their focus away from what you're saying.

Sounding your best

Drink water approximately 20 minutes prior to speaking. Drinking water before you speak will lubricate your vocal cords. Breathing deeply and slowly will allow you to project your voice and pause when you want to - not when you need to. Speak slower that you normally speak. The audience needs to hear you, think about it and internalize it.

Your associate

Always have at least one associate to assist you on the day. This is a simple yet important secret to presentation success. In-person, your associate should sit near the back of the room so they can survey the room, help late arrivals and do things without disturbing the audience. Whether In-person or virtual, they will take care of your logistics, handouts, hosting the participants and room lights or virtual spotlighting and on-screen displays. It is their job to head off problems before they erupt. They should know how to work the room facilities or virtual features, and who to call for help if needed.

TOP TIPS FOR DELIVERING YOUR PRESENTATION

Last minute details during your presentation

Stay on time

Start your presentation on time and finish on time. If you start all your meetings and presentations on time people will learn to show up on time. Do not repeat yourself for latecomers.

If there is a small group at starting time then be prepared to 'start' with a discussion instead of your speech. Those that are there will believe that you started on time and those arriving late will seat themselves quickly feeling a bit guilty for being late.

Finish on time, even if it means leaving something out. For that reason always get your important messages out early. Never keep the key message until the end of your speech. Your audience might have disengaged by that time. Ensure that all devices are switched off, or at least silent, and position a small clock or timer where you can see it so you know where you are in your presentation. Don't make the mistake of asking, "How are we doing for time?" You should know - you are the speaker.

Eye Contact

Talk directly to your audience. The best presentation is delivered as a conversation to every person in the room, one person at a time. If you want to be believed, look every individual in the eye. Don't make the big mistake committed by many novice public speakers by staring at the spot on the back wall. Equally with a virtual presentation, make eye contact by looking directly into your webcam. Imagine your audience is in the room with you, and that you are presenting to each and every person.

Emphasize key points

If you want people to remember something - repeat it at least three times during your speech. The first time they might hear it. The second time they might mull it over. The third time it might stick.

Help your audience remember the important parts

Repeat the points you want them to remember. Use an anecdote or story to illustrate the point. Pause just before and after you state the key points. We find it easier to remember images and feelings. If you want your audience to remember the key points of your presentation attach those points to images or emotions. Men tend to be more visual with memory while women are more emotional. Be sure to address both needs in your presentations.

Correcting things that go wrong

If you look and sound calm the audience will not know that anything is wrong. They might even think that you planned the interruption. When things go wrong, smile, pause, breathe and sound confident. Adapt your presentation. Never appear to panic. Instead focus on your message and what you want them to do.

> *"The trouble with talking too fast is you may say something you haven't thought of yet."*
>
> ANN LANDERS

Introduction to Body Language

Stand Firm

The way you stand when you are presenting before an audience is more important than most people seem to think. I've attended presentations and have been shocked to see the presenter lean against the wall, lean on a desk, and pace the floor over a five- or six-foot path. This type of behavior (though probably unconscious) is extremely distracting.

During an In-person presentation, you should stand with your feet slightly apart – no more than the width of your shoulders. If you have your feet too far apart, you'll appear combative (look at a John Wayne movie to see this stance). On the other hand, you look like a soldier standing at attention if your feet are too close together. And whatever else you do, don't pace the floor. This communicates a feeling of nervousness to the audience.

For a virtual presentation you may stand up, or - most likely - when sitting and presenting to webcam the same guidance applies. Sit tall, feet flat on the floor and avoid movement or twisting in your chair.

Non-Verbal Behavior

Interest in non-verbal behavior is increasing at a rapid rate. That is because:

- By and large people are fascinated by it – so much so, that their expectations about the insights they will gain are often unrealistically high.
- It is widely believed that non-verbal behavior is less easy to bring under conscious control therefore observing and interpreting it gives you a better guide to how someone is actually feeling than their verbal behavior.
- Research shows that non-verbal behaviors do significantly affect communication between people and, despite the difficulties of bringing it under conscious control, non-verbal behaviors can be deliberately avoided or indulged in to improve effectiveness in face-to-face situations.

"Everything becomes a little different as soon as it is spoken out loud."

HERMANN HESSE

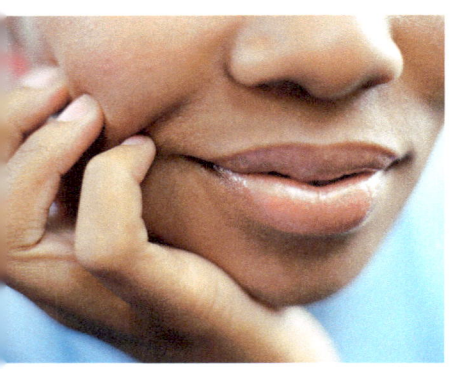

"Be careful of your thoughts; they may become words at any moment."

IRA GASSEN

Audience Non-Verbal Signals

What is your 'audience' doing when you are presenting? The classic things to look for are:

- tilted head - paying attention and enjoying what you say.
- fondling hair - a positive sign - go for a decision.
- resting head on hand - a good sign, they're very interested.
- dilated pupils - a positive sign
- rubs eye - a negative sign. Not 'buying' what you are saying.
- looking down - a very negative sign. Disagreement.
- pinching bridge of nose - trying to decide. You keep quiet.
- rubbing nose - doesn't believe you. Watch it! ("I smell a rat").
- speaking with fingers over mouth - a negative sign, could be lying.

- stroking chin (when trying to decide) - ask questions, then keep quiet.
- folding arms - a defensive negative action. Do not press.
- tapping fingers - impatient. You are probably talking too much.
- steepling fingers - an authoritative gesture. They think they are smarter.
- biting nails - insecure or nervous. Be firm but friendly.
- stroking ear-lobe - a negative sign ("I don't believe what I'm hearing").

"I just wish my mouth had a backspace key."

AUTHOR UNKNOWN

Complete Activity # 6
My Top Tips

ACTIVITY 6: MY TOP TIPS

Select your 3 tips for venue and 'room' control and delivering your presentation. Then record how you will use these techniques to improve presentation success.

My Top Tips	How I will use these techniques to improve presentation success
Venue/'Room' Control	
1.	
2.	
3.	
Presentation Delivery	
1.	
2.	
3.	

Now update your Learning Journal (page 75)

AFTER THE PRESENTATION

Review your presentation and learn from it

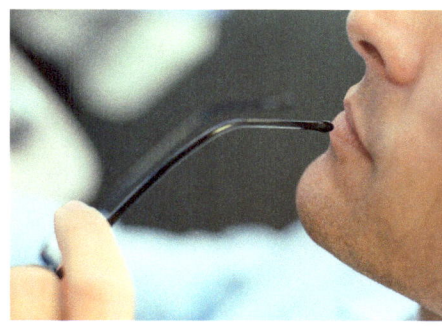

Ask a trusted colleague to attend your presentation and give you constructive feedback. Be specific in what you ask from them; eg "How well was my point illustrated? Did my humor work well? Did I connect with them?" Specific questions will get specific answers.

The most important question you can ask yourself is, "Did I make happen what I wanted to happen?" If the answer is yes – it was a successful presentation. Did they buy, were they convinced, did they march in the direction you pointed, did you communicate what you set out to communicate? That is the measure of a successful speech.

When someone compliments you on the presentation be gracious and ask them, "What was the best idea or strongest message that you will take away and use?" You might be surprised at what they 'heard' versus what you 'said'.

Leverage your presentation

Make your presentation more than an event and part of the process. Summarize key points and questions from the presentation in your newsletter and send a note to everyone. Perhaps the speech would make a good article or blog with some editing.

IN CLOSING...

Public Speaking is a skill. It is not about talent. It is a set of techniques practiced, rehearsed and delivered. You will never deliver the perfect speech. But you might deliver a powerful and effective presentation.

Public speaking is both an art and a science. The more you learn and practice the science the easier the art will work for you. You can be a powerful and effective presenter. It will take time, practice and energy. And those are the elements of greatness.

For success with your presentations:

- **Speak well.**
- **Speak effectively.**
- **Speak with confidence.**
- **Speak to make things happen.**

Section 2
LEARNING JOURNAL

The Learning Journal is used throughout the process to record your key learnings, hot tips and things to remember.

Update your Learning Journal at anytime. Ensure you complete your Learning Journal after you finish each activity. Then turn back to the Learning Short-take® to continue your learning.

LEARNING JOURNAL

As you work through this Learning Short-take®, make detailed notes on this page of the lessons you have learned and any useful skill areas. For each lesson or refresher point think about how you could further develop this skill. Your coach will want to discuss these with you in your Skill Development Action Planning meeting.

"…that is what learning is. You suddenly understand something you've understood all your life, but in a new way."

DORIS LESSING

"Act as though it were impossible to fail."

WINSTON CHURCHILL

"The wise do at once what the fool does later."
BALTASAR GRACIAN (1601-58), SPANISH JESUIT PRIEST AND AUTHOR.

Learning or Idea	Action to be taken	Result Expected

Learning Journal - continued

Learning or Idea	Action to be taken	Result Expected

> *"Anyone who stops learning is old, whether at twenty or eighty."*
> HENRY FORD

Learning or Idea	Action to be taken	Result Expected

"

"There is a difference between wishing for something and being ready to receive it. No one is ready for a thing unless he believes he can acquire it."

NAPOLEON HILL

"

Section 3

SKILL DEVELOPMENT ACTION PLAN

Your Skill Development Action Plan is the last Step in the process. After you have completed the Learning Short-take® and all Activities, update your Learning Journal, then complete this section.

SKILL DEVELOPMENT ACTION PLAN

This is the most important part of the program - your individual Skill Development Action Plan.

You need to complete this plan before meeting with your manager or prior to on-going coaching. You will discuss it in detail with your manager or coach as he or she will ensure that you have everything you need to complete the tasks and activities.

Once you have completed your **Skill Development Action Plan** schedule a meeting time with your manager or coach to review your plan. Take your Learning Short-take® and all other documentation received during the training course to this meeting.

Remember - you have committed to your **Skill Development Action Plan**, and need to make time to complete your tasks!

> *"The mind, once stretched by a new idea, never regains its original dimensions."*
>
> OLIVER WENDELL HOLMES

> *"Whatever you can do or dream you can - begin it. Boldness has genius, power and magic."*
>
> JOHANN WOLFGANG VON GOETHE

"Imagination is the eye of the soul."
JOSEPH JOUBERT (1754-1824)

Task or activity (Be specific)	Measure (this will help you to know you have achieved it)	Date (Be specific)
Reflect on your Learning Journal. Transfer action items that you can apply to your job. Ensure that you include some 'stretch goals' and also a blend of short, medium and long term goals.	Apart from you, who else is needed to assist you in achieving your goal.	Be specific. A general date such as 'Quarter 1', 'August', or 'by end of year' is vague and more likely to result in not achieving your target. Be specific – e.g. 22nd November.

IDEAS FOR DISCUSSION WITH MY MANAGER

Ideas

CONGRATULATIONS!

You've now completed this Learning Short-take®.

Meet with your Manager/Coach to discuss your
Skill Development Action Plan.

> "The only thing we have to fear is fear itself."
>
> FRANKLIN DELANO ROOSEVELT

QUICK REFERENCE

This Quick Reference provides you with a summary of key concepts, models and reference material from Learning Short-takes®. We have also included some quotations to ponder.

Use this section as a quick reference to keep your learning active.

Quick Reference

> **Make thyself a craftsman in speech, for thereby thou shalt gain the upper hand.**

Inscription found in a 3,000-year-old Egyptian tomb

Types of Presentations

Terms	Definitions
Informative Presentations	The purpose of this presentation is to communicate information, facts and data. Stick to the facts and avoid complicated information.
Instructional Presentations	The purpose of this presentation is to give specific directions or orders. Listeners should come away with new knowledge or a new skill.
Attention Grabbing Presentations	The purpose of this presentation is to make people think about a certain problem or situation. You want to arouse the audience's emotions and intellect so that they will be receptive to your point of view.
Persuasive Presentations	The purpose of this presentation is to convince your listeners to accept your proposal. You must present sufficient logic, evidence, and emotion to sway the audience to your viewpoint.
Decision-Making Presentations	The purpose of this presentation is to move your audience to take your suggested action. You must tell the audience what to do and how to do it. You should also let them know what will happen if they don't do what you ask.
Bad News Presentations	The purpose of this presentation is to deliver unfavorable information.

Quick Reference

Adding Interest Throughout the Presentation

- Stories
- Quotes
- Audience participation
- Questions
- Pictures, cartoons and video-clips
- Sound-clips
- Straw polls
- Audience participation exercises
- Quotations
- Props
- Examples
- Analogies
- Statistics
- Your body language
- Changing tone and pitch of your voice

> **The best way to sound like you know what you're talking about is to know what you're talking about.**
>
> — Author Unknown

Quick Reference

(Pilot test, rehearse, and record yourself on video)

Seven Deadly Presentation Mistakes

1. Apologizing in advance.
2. Failing to explain the reasons why the subject has any relevance or value to the audience.
3. Using a presentation designed for one audience – for a different audience.
4. Telling the audience more than they want to know.
5. Showing detailed or irrelevant slides, or only 1-2 very static slides whilst reading a script.
6. Reading verbatim every word on every visual.
7. Failing to rehearse – "it'll be OK on the day!"

Planning Your Presentation

1. Know Your Audience
2. Set a Clear Objective
3. Create Content Overview & Gather Content
4. Develop Content Detail & Create Visual Aids
5. Rehearse
6. Consider Co-/Multi Presenters
7. Evaluate your Presentation

Quick Reference

> **Always be shorter than anybody dared to hope.**

Lord Reading, on speechmaking

Presentation Flow

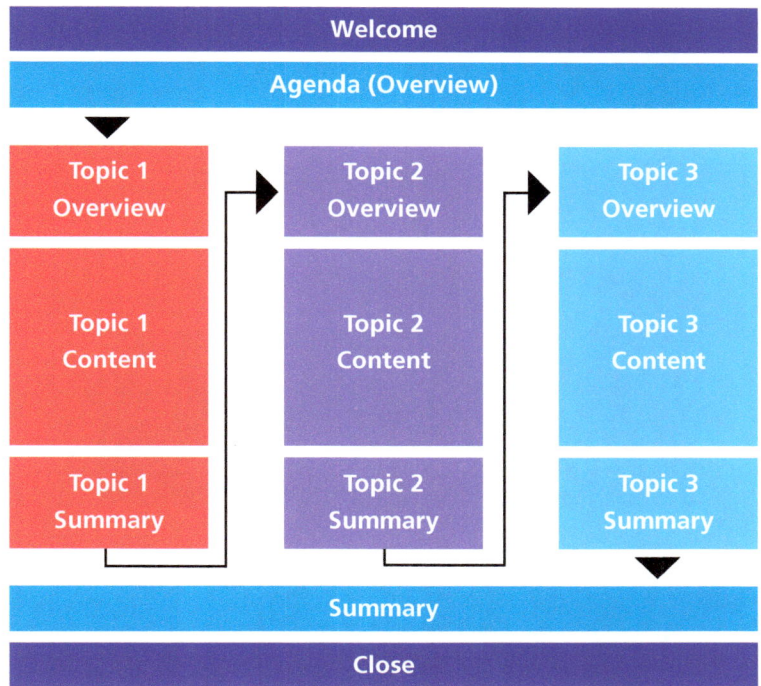

Quick Reference

Sensory Learning

1.0%	taste
1.5%	touch
3.5%	smell
11.0%	hearing
83.0%	sight

> **It usually takes me more than three weeks to prepare a good impromptu speech.**
>
> — Mark Twain

Quick Reference

(Pilot test, rehearse, and record yourself on video)

Reducing Nervousness

Know the material	Accept some fears as being good (energizing stress vs. destructive)
Practice	Introduce yourself
Involve the Audience	Identify your fears
Learn participants' names	Super-prepare the first 5 minutes
Establish credibility early	Practice responses to tough questions
Use eye contact	Imagine yourself as a good speaker
Prepare. Prepare. Prepare	Check facilities, software and tech, and equipment
Anticipate problems	Know the Audience
Be natural	Relax
Ask: "What's in it for the audience	Prepare an outline
Assume they are on your side	Get plenty of rest
Agenda and Summary	Be yourself

 **" I just wish my mouth had a backspace key. "**

Author Unknown

Quick Reference

After the Presentation

- Review your presentation and learn from it
- Leverage your presentation

For Presentation Success

- Speak well.
- Speak effectively.
- Speak with confidence.
- Speak to make things happen.

Quick Reference

> **Be careful of your thoughts; they may become words at any moment.**
>
> Ira Gassen

NEXT STEPS

Congratulations! You have now completed this Learning Short-take® title. The entire list of Learning Short-takes® can be found on the catherinemattiske.com website.

In this section we have suggested Learning Short-take® titles for you that will build your learning. You may order these Learning Short-takes® online at https://www.catherinemattiske.com/books or from your bookstores.

Adult Learning Principles 1
Understanding the Ways Adults Learn

Learning Short-take® Outline

Adult Learning Principles 1 combines self-study with realistic workplace activities for trainers, educators, facilitators and managers to develop skills and knowledge in the principles of adult learning. It will add adult learning techniques to your 'grab bag' of learning design tools for improved learning outcomes. After evaluation of your current approach to learning design, you will learn to develop new and innovative strategies to engage learners at every level. Significantly increasing participant retention and training results **Adult Learning Principles 1** will fuel your confidence in designing successful training workshops and e-Learning every time.

The principles of adult learning work on the basis that we all learn differently, and the way we like to receive and interpret information varies from person to person. Trainers and facilitators who use a combination of adult learning principles to provide balance in their programs increase the chances of keeping all participants focused and engaged throughout the learning process. **Adult Learning Principles 1** will assist you in building a good mix of adult learning styles which is critical in ensuring learning, thorough participant retention and workplace application.

Adult Learning Principles 1 includes the job aid **Strategies for Meeting Global and Specific Needs**, the **Adult Learning Principles Quick Reference Wall Chart and the Activity Booklet**, provided as free downloadable tools.

Learning Objectives

- Successfully match adult learning terms with definitions.
- Determine your personal Learning Style preference.
- List and give working examples of three Adult Learning Principles – Global vs Specific, Learning Styles and Learning Types.
- Develop strategies and ideas to link Adult Learning Principles with Instructional Design.

Course Content

- Part 1: Understanding Adult Learners
- Part 2: Adult Learning Principle 1 - Global vs Specific Learners
- Part 3: Adult Learning Principle 2 - Learning Style - Modalities
- Part 4: Adult Learning Principle 3 - Learning Types - The 4Mat System

Confident Facilitation Skills
Tools and Techniques for the Professional Facilitator

Course Content

- Part 1: The Role of the Facilitator
- Part 2: Preparing for Facilitation
- Part 3: Conducting the Session
- Part 4: Dealing with Difficult Situations
- Part 5: Problem Solving Techniques

Learning Short-take® Outline

Confident Facilitation Skills combines self-study with realistic workplace activities to provide you with the key skills and techniques to become a more effective facilitator. You will be guided through a comprehensive approach to prepare for a facilitation session, focus the group, draw out ideas, manage difficult behavior, build consensus, maintain high energy, close the session, and construct customized agendas. **Confident Facilitation Skills** also includes a comprehensive reference guide of proven group facilitation techniques.

Facilitation is fast becoming a key skill for anyone who is in a team, leading a project team, heading up a working group, or managing a department. Facilitation is the skill and art of guiding others to solve problems to achieve objectives without personally giving advice or offering solutions. A facilitator provides the structure and process - enabling groups to function effectively and make high-quality decisions.

Confident Facilitation Skills includes the **Confident Facilitation Initial Meeting Planning Tool**, provided to you as a free download.

Learning Objectives

- Define the role of a facilitator.
- Identify the key facilitation principles.
- Describe best practices related to each facilitation principle.
- Differentiate between process and content facilitation.
- Identify the core practices and skills required for effective facilitation.
- Explain how to stimulate group participation and positively handle conflict.
- Create a Skill Development Action Plan.

Influencing for Opportunity
Identify and Maximize Ways to Influence

Course Content

- Part 1: Fundamentals of Influence
- Part 2: Influence: A Choice
- Part 3: Naturally Occurring Influence Patterns
- Part 4: Methods of Persuasion
- Part 5: The Challenges of Influence
- Part 6: Building a life of Influence

Learning Short-take® Outline

Influencing for Opportunity combines self-study with realistic workplace activities to provide you with the key skills and techniques to influence those around you. You will learn the theory of influence, influence principles and strategies, as well as how to plan and prepare for important opportunities to influence. As a result, you should achieve greater results in your organization, work more productively and effectively in a team environment, and develop stronger working relationships with co-workers, suppliers and customers.

The ability to influence others is critical in today's competitive business environment. Being highly skilled in influence enables you to build the relationships you need to get results inside or outside the organization. Employees and managers alike cannot assume they have power over others - they must earn it through influence. Being an influential person is a skill that can be learned and practiced. **Influencing for Opportunity** will help you succeed in the modern corporate environment by increasing your ability to influence others.

Influencing for Opportunity includes a **toolkit of job aids and learning support tools** provided to you as free downloads.

Learning Objectives

- Identify patterns of influence.
- Evaluate how you currently use influence behaviors and identify areas for development.
- Develop influence behaviors for greater personal and business success.
- Establish clear and powerful influence goals.
- Increase influence to overcome resistance.
- Describe how to ask for and receive support.
- Design an approach for formal and informal influence situations; apply the approach to a real-life situation.
- Create a Skill Development Action Plan.

www.catherinemattiske.com

www.ingramcontent.com/pod-product-compliance
Lightning Source LLC
Chambersburg PA
CBHW042230090526
44587CB00001B/15